MYSTERIES UNWRAPPED:
MEDICAL MARVELS

WRITTEN BY
GEORGE E. STANLEY

ILLUSTRATED BY
JOSH COCHRAN

STERLING

New York / London
www.sterlingpublishing.com/kids

STERLING and the distinctive Sterling logo are registered
trademarks of Sterling Publishing Co., Inc.

Library of Congress Cataloging-in-Publication Data

Stanley, George Edward.
  Mysteries unwrapped. Medical marvels / written by George Edward
Stanley ; illustrated by Josh Cochran.
    p. cm.
  Includes bibliographical references and index.
  ISBN 978-1-4027-3930-9
  1. Medicine--Miscellanea--Juvenile literature. I. Cochran, Josh, ill.
II. Title. III. Title: Medical marvels.
  R706.S736 2009   610--dc22

                                                2009003777

10 9 8 7 6 5 4 3 2 1

Published by Sterling Publishing Co., Inc.
387 Park Avenue South, New York, NY 10016
Text © 2009 by George Edward Stanley
Illustrations © 2009 by Josh Cochran
Distributed in Canada by Sterling Publishing
c/o Canadian Manda Group, 165 Dufferin Street
Toronto, Ontario, Canada M6K 3H6
Distributed in the United Kingdom by GMC Distribution Services
Castle Place, 166 High Street, Lewes, East Sussex, England BN7 1XU
Distributed in Australia by Capricorn Link (Australia) Pty. Ltd.
P.O. Box 704, Windsor, NSW 2756, Australia

Printed in China
Sterling ISBN 978-1-4027-3930-9

Book design by Josh Moore of beardandglasses.com

For information about custom editions, special sales, premium and
corporate purchases, please contact Sterling Special Sales
Department at 800-805-5489 or specialsales@sterlingpublishing.com.

SINCE THE DAWN OF HISTORY, HUMANS HAVE SUFFERED FROM AILMENTS WITH STRANGE, MYSTERIOUS, AND SOMETIMES DOWNRIGHT GROSS SYMPTOMS.
—NANCY BUTCHER

CONTENTS

INTRODUCTION

Detective stories prove that sometimes the most fun can be had by chasing down the unknown. Detectives hunt for clues, talk to eyewitnesses, and piece information together in the hope of revealing the truth and solving the mystery. In the world of medicine—past and present—marvelous mysteries abound. This book will guide you through some of the most surprising and curious terrain that medical science has to offer.

Begin your investigation by getting to know three people who became international celebrities by performing in so-called freak shows. Sure, each one stood out in a crowd, but dig a little deeper and you may be surprised to find a set of twins who just wanted to settle down, raise a family, and work on a farm. Then pack your bags and head into the remote forests of Uganda, the seventeenth-century French countryside, and the flat expanses of the Sahara, where you'll meet some children so wild that they may leave you scratching your head and looking for evidence. From there, get lost in the dizzying back alleyways of your own mind as you explore the brain. Stop off for an immunization before trying to spot the killer in the police lineup of deadly viruses in Chapter 4. Finally, bring the investigation back home by searching yourself for clues to a few common medical marvels.

Proceed cautiously through the pages that follow. Be armed with consideration and curiosity, a sense of adventure, a willingness to be surprised, and a hazmat suit, if you have one on hand.

CIRCUS CHARADE: RARE MEDICAL CONDITIONS

1.

Throughout history, people all over the world have gone to circuses, carnivals, and "freak shows" to gawk at people or animals that seem odd or different. As far back as the 1630s the Italian conjoined twins Lazarus Colloredo and Joannes Baptista Colloredo traveled throughout Europe to earn money. Joannes's upper body was connected and jutted out from his brother Lazarus's sternum. That unexplained sight astounded audiences. Even the famous Russian ruler Peter the Great collected oddities and housed them in the first Russian museum, which was called "the Kunstkamera."

In the United States, freak shows had their heyday from the 1840s through the 1940s. The famous showman and circus boss P.T. Barnum made his fortune exhibiting curiosities and live acts. His attractions ranged from individuals with rare physical conditions—albinos (people who lack skin color), bearded ladies, little people, obese people—to performers such as jugglers and magicians. He also included unconventional figures, such as people who were heavily tattooed, as well as performing animals.

The freak show was a popular form of entertainment and evolved to include fire eaters, sword swallowers, contortionists,

KUNSTKAMERA

The Kunstkamera was Russia's first museum. It was opened in 1714 in St. Petersburg by the tsar, or Russian emperor, Peter the Great. Peter wanted a place to store his vast collection of rare objects, which included a large assortment of ancient weapons and utensils as well as animal and human fetuses with anatomic deformities.

In 1717, Peter decided to expand his collection for the benefit of the public. He sent out an announcement that people should send him anything unusual they had in their possession so that he could display it in the museum. Soon, from all over the country, various oddities began to arrive: a sheep with two tongues and two sets of eyes on each side of its head, a lamb with eight legs. In fact, so many specimens poured into St. Petersburg that Peter was forced to relocate the museum to a larger space. He eventually constructed a special building in the center of the capital.

In addition to displays of rare butterflies, stuffed animals—such as lizards and elephants—ancient manuscripts, and Roman coins, there were "live" exhibits of people with uncommon physical features such as deformed hands and feet. When those "living exhibits" died, their skeletons, along with specimens of their organs preserved in jars, were put on display. Today it's considered inhumane to exhibit live humans, but popular opinion was different at that point in history and Peter saw nothing wrong with exhibiting people who had been born with what were called "artistic human creations." During the 1830s, many of the Kunstkamera's displays were moved to other museums, but much of the original collection is still on view.

and any number of spectacles designed to shock or interest the crowd. Many of the shocking attractions were actually hoaxes, or frauds. Showmen often lied to boost ticket sales and attract people to their shows.

Times have changed, and today it's considered cruel to call someone a "freak" or, worse, exhibit that person in a show to earn money. Although some of the people who participated in freak shows and circuses did so willingly or went along with it to support themselves, many more were mistreated.

Freak shows also lost their appeal because advances in science and medicine made it possible to explain what once had been unexplainable. We now know more about the rare but totally natural conditions that often lead to extreme physical differences—often called "medical anomalies." We know, for instance, that very tall people are not magical beings or ogres. Instead, we can assume that genetic factors or pituitary gland problems produce extreme tallness.

Here are the true stories and the fascinating facts behind some of history's most famous medical anomalies.

JO-JO THE DOG-FACED BOY

Everyone thought Fedor Jeftichew was a werewolf, or worse. They called him "Jo-Jo the Dog-Faced Boy." But Fedor was no werewolf—he just had hypertrichosis.

Hypertrichosis is a disorder that causes thick hair to grow all over a person's body, including the face. Before people knew about hypertrichosis, they often were frightened by humans with so much hair. The legend of the werewolf, a creature that is

This photograph of P.T. Barnum was taken sometime between 1855 and 1865.

In this photograph from 1938, spectators crowd around to see the circus side show at an Ohio county fair. (COURTESY LIBRARY OF CONGRESS)

half man and half wolf, probably was invented to help explain people like Fedor before medical answers were discovered.

Unsurprisingly, hypertrichosis also is called "Werewolf Syndrome." The condition usually produces hair on every portion of the skin except the palms of hands and the soles of the feet. The density, thickness, rate of growth, texture, and color of the hair vary from person to person. All these qualities, as well as the condition of hypertrichosis itself, are passed from one generation to the next through genes, the mechanism for heredity. Severe hypertrichosis is rare, and Fedor's hypertrichosis was severe.

Fedor was born in Russia in 1868. His father, Adrian, passed the condition on to his son. In 1884, P.T. Barnum brought Fedor and his father to the United States so that they could appear in his circus. Barnum put Fedor on display and told spectators that a hunter had tracked Fedor and his father to their cave and captured them. Barnum cautioned that Fedor and his father were so savage that they could never be civilized. That wasn't true, of course—Fedor was quite intelligent and able to speak three languages: Russian, German, and English—but Barnum wanted to lead his audiences to believe that he'd captured real werewolves. He also bragged to the crowds that when Fedor was upset, he would growl and bark like a dog. Thus, during each show, Fedor acted like a savage to earn money and draw crowds. And it worked—at the height of his celebrity in the 1880s he performed approximately twenty-three shows per day.

The advertisement describing "Jo-Jo" was purely sensational:

By special permit from the Czar of all the Russias, we exhibit for the first and only time in the New World. The most prodigious paragon of all prodigies secured by P.T. Barnum in over 50 years. The human-skye terrier the crowning mystery of nature's Contradictions. The incarnate paradox, before which Science stands confounded and blindly wonders, was found about thirteen years ago in company with his Dog-Faced father, living in a remote cave in deep Kostroma Forests of Central Russia. They were first discovered by a hunter, and a party was formed who tracked them to their cave, and, after a desperate conflict, in which the savage father fought with all the fury of an enraged mastiff, their capture was effected. . . .

Fedor toured the United States and Europe extensively. He eventually married and had a son who also had hypertrichosis.

This photograph of Fedor Jeftichew, better known as "Jo-Jo the Dog-Faced Boy," was taken c. 1890. (THE GRANGER COLLECTION, NEW YORK)

But his life in show business was cut short at the early age of thirty-six when he died of pneumonia on January 31, 1904, in Salonica (now a part of Greece).

CHANG AND ENG

There are many different types of twins, but there was only one set like the famous brothers Chang and Eng.

Fraternal and identical twins are quite common. Fraternal twins occur when two separate eggs are fertilized by two different sperm. Identical twins occur when a single fertilized egg splits and develops into two fetuses. Sometimes, though, identical twins fail to separate completely into two individuals—they remain connected. When these babies are born, they are called "conjoined twins." Statistically, conjoined twins are rare, occurring only once in approximately 250,000 live births. Conjoined twins usually are joined at the chest, the head, or the pelvis. In some instances, conjoined twins share one or more internal organs. Surgical separation of the twins is sometimes possible, but that depends on where the twins are joined and which organs they share

The most famous conjoined twins were Chang and Eng Bunker, who were born on May 11, 1811, in Siam (present-day Thailand). They were connected at the chest by a five-inch-wide band of flesh. At the time, the location of that connection caused doctors to believe that the brothers shared a heart or some respiratory functions and that trying to separate them would kill one or both of the twins. Today, it is known that they could have been separated, although nineteenth-century physicians did not have the knowledge or technology to do so.

STATISTICALLY, CONJOINED TWINS ARE RARE, OCCURRING ONLY ONCE IN APPROXIMATELY 250,000 LIVE BIRTHS. CONJOINED TWINS USUALLY ARE JOINED AT THE CHEST, THE HEAD, OR THE PELVIS. IN SOME INSTANCES, CONJOINED TWINS SHARE ONE OR MORE INTERNAL ORGANS.

As boys in Siam, Chang and Eng played with other children, did their household chores, and helped support their family by gathering and selling wild duck eggs in their village. They functioned remarkably well as a unit and were perfectly capable of taking care of themselves. They could run and swim—later in life they even became expert marksmen. When Chang and Eng were teenagers, they met two British merchants, Robert Hunter and Abel Coffin, who convinced the twins that they could make a lot of money by touring the world so that curious people could come see them. For the next several years, they traveled to the United States, Canada, South America, and Europe, promoting themselves as "Siamese twins," a term that was used for many years to describe connected or conjoined twins. When Chang and Eng completed their contractual obligations with Hunter and Coffin, they decided to go into business for themselves and made a small fortune touring their act.

By 1839, Chang and Eng were tired of the constant travel and decided to settle in Wilkesboro, North Carolina. They purchased a 1,000-acre plantation and thirty-three slaves. As a part of the process of becoming Americans, they adopted the last name Bunker. They wanted to put show business behind them and farm for a living. In 1843, they married two sisters, Adelaide and Sarah Anne Yates, who were neither twins nor conjoined. Between them, they produced twenty-one children and lived together in a single home. Eventually, squabbling between the two wives forced Chang and Eng to set up different households. The twins would alternate residences, spending three days at a time at each home.

Chang and Eng, the famous "Siamese twins," pose for this photograph taken by Mathew Brady c. 1865. (GETTY IMAGES)

Although Chang and Eng previously had had very little contact with the most famous showman of the time, P.T. Barnum, in 1860 they allowed him to display a wax figure of their likeness in his museum, Barnum's American Museum in Manhattan. During the American Civil War, Chang's son Christopher and Eng's son Stephen both fought for the South. When the Union forces in the North won the war, Chang and Eng—along with other plantation owners in the South—suffered enormous financial loses. To make money, the twins agreed to participate in a European tour sponsored by Barnum in 1868.

In 1870, back at home after their tour with Barnum, Chang had a stroke, and his health declined steadily. Four years later, in January 1874, Chang and Eng died during the night. They were sixty-three years old. Chang's death occurred almost three hours

P.T. BARNUM

P.T. Barnum was an American showman who gained worldwide recognition for his exhibits of humans with rare physical deformities. He also formed the world's most famous circus: the Ringling Bros. and Barnum & Bailey Circus. In 1841, Barnum bought the American Museum in New York City and turned it into an exhibition hall and showplace for everything from "the Feejee Mermaid" (thought to be a mummified monkey and fish fused to resemble a mermaid) to the diminutive performer General Thom Thumb.

P.T. Barnum was a brilliant showman because he had a knack for spotting— or, in some cases, manufacturing—crowd-pleasing attractions. Among his many successful acts were the Swedish opera singer Jenny Lind, Jumbo the elephant, and Chang and Eng Bunker, the conjoined twins.

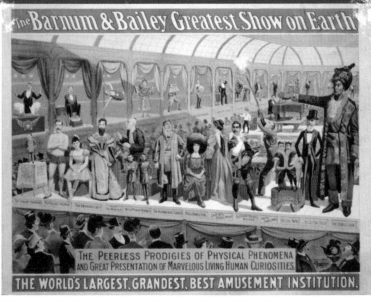

This poster for the Barnum & Bailey Circus from 1898 advertises a few of the show's amazing attractions, including the "Smallest Man Alive" and "the Congo Giant." (Courtesy Library of Congress)

before Eng's. Later, an autopsy showed that Chang had died of a blood clot in the brain. Eng's death was attributed to shock.

THE ELEPHANT MAN

Joseph Carey Merrick was born in England in 1862 and became known as "the Elephant Man" because people thought he had a condition known as "elephantiasis." Merrick was disfigured by a disorder that caused abnormal masses of flesh to grow on his face and body. The outline of Merrick's head grew as large as three feet around, and because his bone structure also was affected, he could not show facial expressions and had difficulty speaking. His right hand was enlarged and finlike, but his left arm was not affected. Merrick needed a cane to walk because one hip and both legs were deformed.

Recent DNA and X-ray tests on Merrick's hair and bones have shown that he actually had what is called "Proteus syndrome" (named for the mythological shape-shifting Greek god Proteus). This disorder causes excessive growth of skin, bones, muscles, and fatty tissues; that is why people often confuse it with elephantiasis. Proteus syndrome develops over time. People with the condition often show no signs at birth, but the symptoms surface gradually as they age. Proteus syndrome is considered a sporadic rather than a familial disorder, meaning that it isn't passed down from generation to generation.

Merrick began to show signs of Proteus syndrome when he was two years old. When his mother died, Merrick was sent to live with his father, but Merrick's stepmother treated him badly and forced him to become a street peddler. Because of his

WHAT IS ELEPHANTIASIS?

Elephantiasis, or lymphatic filariasis—the disease Merrick was falsely diagnosed with—causes parts of a person's body, especially the arms and legs, to grow to several times the average size. Sometimes this disease also affects internal organs such as the kidneys and the lymphatic system.

Over 120 million people have been affected by the condition, and 40 million of them have been seriously disfigured and incapacitated. One-third of the people with the disease live in India, one-third in Africa, and the remaining one-third in southern Asia, the Pacific islands, and the Americas.

The disease is spread by infected mosquitoes that transmit a threadlike parasitic worm into the bloodstream. The development of the disease is still something of a mystery to scientists. Although the infection generally is acquired early in childhood, it may take years to emerge. Today, simple early detection tests along with new medical treatments have given hope to many patients.

deformities, it was difficult for Merrick to find employment. Finally, as a last resort, he took a job in a circus sideshow. When those shows were outlawed in England in 1886 by socially conscious politicians, Merrick went to Belgium. He found work but was treated badly and eventually abandoned by cruel and dishonest circus owners.

Back home in England, Merrick was befriended by an influential British physician, Dr. Frederick Treves. Under Dr. Treves's care, Merrick was given a permanent home in the London Hospital and introduced to wealthy people who took an interest in him. His reputation grew, and he became an unlikely celebrity—he even became friendly with the queen of England, Queen Victoria.

Despite the good care Merrick received at the hospital, he died on April 11, 1890, at the age of twenty-seven. Merrick was unable to recline while he slept, as most people do, because of the size and weight of his head. It is thought that he might have suffocated accidentally in an effort to sleep lying down. Merrick's preserved skeleton is on permanent display at the Royal London Hospital.

This photograph of Joseph Carey Merrick, better known as "the Elephant Man," was taken c. 1889.

(© ROYAL LONDON HOSPITAL ARCHIVES)

MERRICK WAS GIVEN A PERMANENT HOME IN THE LONDON HOSPITAL AND INTRODUCED TO WEALTHY PEOPLE WHO TOOK AN INTEREST IN HIM. HE BECAME AN UNLIKELY CELEBRITY—HE EVEN BECAME FRIENDLY WITH THE QUEEN OF ENGLAND, QUEEN VICTORIA.

2. BORN TO BE WILD: FERAL CHILDREN

In *The Jungle Book* by Rudyard Kipling, the character Mowgli was raised by wolves in the jungles of India. He was separated from his parents during a tiger attack when he was a baby and adopted by a wolf pack that saved his life by teaching him (as did other animal friends) how to hunt and track. Here's how Kipling described Mowgli's lessons:

> . . . Baloo [a bear, Mowgli's friend and mentor] was teaching him the Law of the Jungle. The big, serious, old brown bear was delighted to have so quick a pupil, for the young wolves will only learn as much of the Law of the Jungle as applies to their own pack and tribe. . . . But Mowgli, as a man-cub, had to learn a great deal more than this. . . . The boy could climb almost as well as he could swim, and swim almost as well as he could run; so Baloo, the Teacher of the Law, taught him the Wood and Water laws: how to tell a rotten branch from a sound one; how to speak politely to the wild bees when he came upon a hive of them fifty feet above-ground; what to say to Mang, the Bat, when he disturbed him in the branches at midday; and how to warn the water-snakes in the pools before he splashed down among them. . . .

This illustration depicts the character Mowgli from Rudyard Kipling's collection of stories *The Jungle Book*. Mowgli is shown sitting with his adopted animal family.
(THE GRANGER COLLECTION, NEW YORK)

All this will show you how much Mowgli had to learn by heart, and ... as Baloo said ... : "A man's cub is a man's cub, and he must learn all the Law of the Jungle."

Mowgli's story is fiction, but there are astonishing stories about feral children said to exist in the real world. A feral child is one who is born into civilization but for any of a number of reasons is separated and isolated from human contact. The stories that follow are about children who've gone, well . . . WILD.

THE MONKEY BOY OF UGANDA

In 1991, Milly Sseba, a tribeswoman from a small village in Uganda, East Africa, went out into the forest to gather kindling for the cooking fire and was startled by the sight of a young boy hiding in a tree. She quickly ran back to the village and told some of the tribal elders about it. The men went out and found the boy, but he resisted their efforts to bring him back to the village. Within minutes, a band of vervet monkeys rushed to the boy's defense and began throwing branches at the villagers. When the boy finally was captured, the villagers cleaned him up and discovered that his body was covered with scars and wounds. His knees, particularly, showed signs of wear, and the villagers thought that might be evidence that he'd been crawling instead of walking on two legs.

Eventually, the boy, who initially could neither talk nor cry, was put in the care of Paul and Molly Wasswa, who ran a charitable foundation for orphans. Over time, the boy began to speak, and his story slowly came to light. He was identified as John Ssebunya, who lived in the village of Kabonge, north of the Ugandan capital of Kampala. In 1989, after witnessing horrible violence at home, four-year-old John ran and hid in the forest that surrounded his village, fearing for his life. He was so afraid of his father that he decided to remain in the forest. Some of his caretakers suspected that he was so upset and scared that he didn't trust adults enough to seek help.

Residents of nearby villages, when questioned, reported that from time to time they had caught glimpses of John in the trees. He seemed so wild that they didn't try to capture him. John was discovered during a terrible time of strife in Uganda. Civil war raged under the military dictator and president, Idi Amin. There was a lot of confusion and disorder as villagers relocated to safer areas—away from warring tribes and Amin's military. Out of fear, many people chose to keep to themselves. But something made Milly Sseba want to rescue John. As it turned out, he was lucky she did because he was severely malnourished and needed

FERAL CHILDREN HOAXES

Many stories about feral children turn out to be untrue. Here are two infamous tales:

In 1997, Misha Defonseca wrote a best-selling book about her experiences during World War II. According to Defonseca, in 1941, when she was six years old, she was rescued at her school in Belgium after her parents were arrested and deported by the Nazis. She was sent to live with another family and given the name Monique. Unhappy with her new family, she ran away, hoping to find her parents. Over the next four years she wandered alone across Germany, Poland, the Ukraine, Romania, and Yugoslavia. On the east coast of Yugoslavia, she stowed away on a boat bound for Italy and then walked up through Italy, across the Alps, to France and finally back to Belgium. During that time, Monique claimed she found shelter with packs of wolves, killed a German soldier, and wandered mistakenly into the Jewish ghetto in Warsaw, where she barely escaped, before she returned home. When writers at the *Boston Globe* began to question the truth of Defonseca's story, it slowly started to unravel. Finally, in February 2008 Defonseca admitted that she had made everything up. Her real name was Monique De Wael and her parents had been arrested by the Nazis, but she had been sent to live with her grandfather. She wandered across Europe only in her imagination.

In 1976, Harlan Lane read an article in the *Johannesburg* (South Africa) *Times* about a boy from Burundi (East Africa) who had been raised by monkeys. Lane, who was considered an expert on feral children, thought this would be an excellent opportunity to research a story firsthand instead of having to rely on written records. Lane, accompanied by Richard Pillard, a psychiatrist from Boston University, headed for Burundi, but their investigation revealed that the boy had early childhood autism and was severely disabled. They discovered that both of the boy's parents had died and he had been shuffled around to various orphanages. His identify was never established, but it was apparent that he had never lived with monkeys. Lane and Pillard wrote about their investigation in a 1979 book called *The Wild Boy of Burundi*, which told the sad tale of the boy's childhood.

John Ssebunya lived among African vervet monkeys like the ones in this photograph. (© iStockphoto.com / "*Laila Kazakevica*")

to be treated for parasitic worms. If he hadn't been rescued, he probably would have died within a few weeks.

Most Ugandans consider monkeys to be pests because they destroy crops. People usually chase them away or destroy them on sight, but the civil war caused people to pay less attention to monkeys, and their numbers increased dramatically. After John learned to speak, he told how he had come across a group of vervet monkeys in the forest that raided the crops of villagers—stealing bananas, cassava, and yams. He recounted how they offered him some of their food.

Scientist who study primates (humans, apes, and monkeys) have disputed that, saying that it is unlikely the monkeys actually *offered* John food but that it wouldn't be unusual for the monkeys to steal more food than they could eat. They suspect that the monkeys dropped what they didn't want on the ground and allowed John to eat their leftovers. The fact that John identified the monkeys as vervet, the common African gray monkey, made his story more believable. Vervets are one of the few species of mammals that live in social groups and will not only tolerate but usually accept another species of monkey—or, in John's case, a small human being—living alongside their group. Most monkeys and apes will not allow that living arrangement.

Dr. Debbie Cox, an Australian primatologist, was working with the Uganda Wild Life and Education Center in the city of Entebbe and had a chance to observe John as he interacted with a group of African gray monkeys. She wrote that she had never witnessed an untrained individual who could interact and communicate with the monkeys to the degree that John could. Her observations added credibility to John Ssebunya's story. Dr. Cox added that even Ugandan children who had monkeys as pets never learned the animals' social behavior patterns. She believes that John developed his familiarity with the monkeys by living with a group of them over an extended period. John was not reared by monkeys, as in the movie *Tarzan,* nor was he stolen as a baby. At most, he lived alongside the monkeys and was tolerated and accepted.

With the care John received in the orphanage, he was able to resume a life in society. He not only learned to talk, he also learned to sing and went on tour with the Pearl of Africa Children's Choir.

THE FACT THAT
JOHN IDENTIFIED
THE MONKEYS AS
VERVET, THE COMMON
AFRICAN GRAY MONKEY,
MADE HIS STORY
MORE BELIEVABLE.

In October 1999, John was the subject of a BBC documentary called "Living Proof." Today, John continues his work with the orphanage that originally took him in, trying to make sure that other Ugandan children are as fortunate as he was.

WILD GIRL OF CHAMPAGNE— MARIE-ANGÉLIQUE MEMMIE LE BLANC

In 1731, French peasants near the village of Songy in northeastern France were startled by a noise in a tree. When they looked up, they saw what they first thought was a wild animal. But when they finally coaxed the creature down, they discovered that it was a *human*—it turned out to be a young woman!

She was dressed in rags and animal skins. Instead of talking, she shrieked, squeaked, and made other animal-like sounds. She was so dirty that the peasants thought she was black and somehow had traveled from North Africa to France. For food, she ate birds, frogs, and fish—raw! When the peasants gave her a rabbit, she immediately skinned it and ate it. According to the famous French scientist Charles Marie de la Condamine, the "wild girl of Champagne," as she later was named, had incredibly sharp eyesight and could run very fast.

Eventually, the girl was given the name Marie-Angélique Memmie Le Blanc and taken to Paris. It took over 200 years for pieces of her story to emerge. The American scholar Julia Douthwaite and the French surgeon Serge Aroles unearthed hundreds of documents on Marie-Angélique. They discovered

SHE WAS DRESSED IN RAGS AND ANIMAL SKINS. INSTEAD OF TALKING, SHE SHRIEKED, SQUEAKED, AND MADE OTHER ANIMAL-LIKE SOUNDS. FOR FOOD, SHE ATE BIRDS, FROGS, AND FISH—RAW!

FOX TRIBE

The Native American tribe called the Meskwaki, meaning "red earth people," is one of several tribes that originally inhabited the eastern woodlands and prairies of Michigan and Wisconsin. The French fur traders who moved into the area in the early 1700s renamed the tribe Fox because they associated their hunting methods with that animal. The Fox controlled most of the waterways in the area and used birch bark canoes (the bark from birch trees stretched over a wooden frame) to navigate the rivers and creeks.

The French wanted to explore the Fox territory to trap animals for fur, but the tribe resisted. The Fox stood their ground against the French attack, but their population was reduced severely by sickness, and they were defeated. Those who were able to escape headed to Sauk (meaning "yellow earth people") villages for protection. The Meskwaki and the Sauk were related to each other and spoke the same language, but politically they were independent. The two tribes eventually merged, and today they live mostly in Iowa, Kansas, and Oklahoma and are known as the Sac and Fox tribe.

that she had been born in approximately 1712 and reared in the Fox tribe, a Native American nation in what is now the state of Wisconsin. The skills she gained as a member of the tribe are probably what saved her and allowed her to survive on her own for ten years (from November 1721 to September 1731) in the forests of France.

During Marie's childhood the tribe's territory was part of French North America. In 1716, the French defeated the Fox at a battle that took place approximately 100 miles west of what is now the city of Chicago, Illinois. Marie-Angélique, along with many other children of the Fox tribe, was sold into slavery and ended up as a servant in the French part of Canada. A wealthy Frenchwoman, Madame de Courtemanche, bought the girl in 1718, took her to a colony called Labrador, and treated her more like a daughter than a servant. How Marie-Angélique left Labrador, though, is still unclear, and different explanations exist. Some historians believe that she was kidnapped and taken to the West Indies by unknown persons who planned to sell her there. Later, Marie-Angélique would tell stories of about huge sugarcane fields; that seemed to confirm the fact that she had been taken to an island in the Caribbean.

However, another theory suggests that Marie traveled back to Europe with Madame de Courtemanche because of conflicts between the Labrador colony and the Inuit, a Native American tribe that shared the territory. After months of strife, members of the colony sailed back to France on September 11, 1721. The ship docked at the port of Marseille on France's Mediterranean coast on

October 20, but when they arrived, they found that the continent was battling a widespread outbreak of plague, a deadly infectious disease. Half of the population of Marseille had died. By leaving the ship, the passengers would have risked infection and death.

After remaining isolated, or quarantined, on the ship for a while with some of the other passengers, Marie-Angélique escaped into the forests of Provence. She was nine years old at the time and spent the next ten years living on her own in the woods.

After Marie-Angélique was discovered by the peasants and taken to Paris, she was hospitalized and finally taken to live in a convent. Attempts to switch her from raw food to cooked food were never completely successful. The Duke of Orléans and many other wealthy and powerful people became her friends. Still, she seemed happiest when she was allowed to wander through the nearby woods. She died at the age of sixty-three on December 15, 1775.

THE GAZELLE BOY OF THE SAHARA

In 1960, a French anthropologist, Jean-Claude Armen, was traveling through an area called Rio de Oro (present-day Western Sahara on the northwest coast of Africa) when he encountered some men herding cattle. They told him about a "wild child" who was only a day's journey away.

The next day, following the men's directions, Armen came upon a naked child galloping among a herd of white gazelles. Gazelles, known for being swift and graceful, are part of the antelope family. They stand approximately two to three feet high at the shoulder and graze in open plains and partial desert lands. Armen knew of a small oasis nearby and, thinking the herd

eventually would go there for water, traveled ahead and waited for them. Three days later, the herd did show up, but it took several more days of waiting patiently before the gazelles, including the young boy, felt safe enough to approach Armen.

Armen estimated the boy's age at about ten years old. The anthropologist noticed that the boy's leg muscles were firm and looked powerful—they would have to be to keep up with the fast and nimble gazelle herd. Although the gazelle boy walked on all fours, he occasionally would stand upright, which made Armen think that before the boy was abandoned, he had learned to stand. Using this reasoning, Armen figured that the boy must not have been abandoned until he was at least ten or eleven months old.

Armen spent several months studying the gazelle boy, who lost his fear of the anthropologist over time. Eventually, Armen came to understand every gesture and movement that the boy shared with the herd. The gazelle boy constantly twitched his muscles, nose, and ears, just like the rest of the gazelles, every time he heard the slightest noise. Even while sleeping, he seemed alert to the slightest sound. Armen noticed that one female gazelle seemed to act as the boy's mother. For food the gazelle boy ate desert roots with the rest of the herd, although he'd occasionally eat a worm or a lizard.

Two years after his initial contact with the gazelle boy, Armen returned with a French military captain. At first they kept their distance from the herd, not wanting to frighten the gazelles, but they wanted to test the boy's speed and eventually used their jeep to track him as he ran. It's alleged that he reached speeds of

THE GAZELLE BOY
CONSTANTLY TWITCHED
HIS MUSCLES, NOSE,
AND EARS, JUST LIKE
THE REST OF THE
GAZELLES, EVERY TIME
HE HEARD THE SLIGHTEST
NOISE. EVEN WHILE
SLEEPING, HE SEEMED
ALERT TO THE SLIGHTEST
SOUND.

A herd of African gazelle, like the one Armen tracked, are grazing in this photograph. (© iStockphoto.com / "*Ali Taylor*")

almost thirty-four miles per hour and could leap thirteen feet. However, because of a flat tire on the jeep, Armen and the captain lost the herd.

In 1966, Armen tried to capture the gazelle boy with the help of American officers from a nearby base. They used a net from a helicopter, but their attempts to capture the gazelle boy were unsuccessful. Final attempts were made during the months of June and July in 1970, but both efforts come up empty. Armen never saw the gazelle boy after that. He wrote about his experiences in a book called *Gazelle-Boy—Beautiful, Astonishing and True—A Wild Boy's Life in the Sahara*. It was first published in Switzerland in 1971 by Delachaux et Niestlé.

WILD CHILDREN OR PERHAPS JUST WILD IMAGINATIONS

There are countless stories about feral children. Some date back hundreds of years, and some, like that of John Ssebunya, are more recent and better documented. Most reports of feral children cannot be authenticated, and historians now believe that the vast majority of these cases were hoaxes. In this chapter, we've made every effort to report facts, but the reader should approach the topic with a healthy dose of skepticism. It's also important not to lose sight of that fact that these children, however fascinating their stories are, should have been under the care of trusted adults. So instead of packing your bags to go live with a band of wild monkeys, consider visiting the zoo instead.

3.

MARVELOUS MACHINE: THE BRAIN

The human brain is like a supercomputer, only better. It has billions of individual pieces and trillions of different connections, weighs about three pounds, and runs on electrochemical energy. To the naked eye, it's nothing more than a lump of pink tissue, but somehow all the pieces are put together just right—enabling us to sleep, eat, laugh, read, breathe, and do everything else we do every day. Let's take a closer look at this marvelous machine.

THE BRAIN IN SLEEP MODE

The brain is active even when the body is asleep. The brain is responsible for the sounds, feelings, and images that are created during dreams. It's still unknown why the brain continues to function while the body is at rest—or why human beings dream at all. Researchers seek to uncover this mystery, and their work, the scientific study of dreams, is called "oneirology." Dreaming has been associated with what is called "rapid eye movement," or REM, which is a normal stage that is part of body function during sleep. Scientists

PHRENOLOGY

During the nineteenth century, phrenology was an extremely popular field of study that was used to analyze the personality traits of individuals by "reading" the bumps on a person's head—almost like reading a palm. Phrenology was developed by Franz Joseph Gall, a German doctor who believed that there were twenty-seven "brain organs" that were responsible for everything from our ability to sense color and remember words to our inclination to be kind and gentle or to commit murder. Gall believed that each bump and pit on a person's skull corresponded to his "brain map," which identified the location of each brain organ inside a person's head.

Here's how it worked: phrenologists would run their fingers over a patient's head to determine his or her psychological qualities and behavior patterns. If a bump was particularly large, it meant that the person used the corresponding organ a lot. When the composer Joseph Haydn died in 1809, a group of phrenologists stole his head from his grave so that they could "read" it. Those men thought that by studying the bumps and indentations on the composer's head, they would be able to discover which brain organs were responsible for his musical genius. (There is no record of any unusual findings.) At the height of its popularity, from 1820 to 1840, parents took their children to phrenologists to find out what their futures would hold—especially what type of person a child should marry.

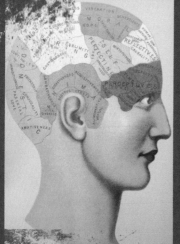

We now know that there is no scientific evidence to support the study of phrenology. We have determined that certain areas of the brain correspond to different functions, but the brain is not composed of twenty-seven organs, and the shape of a person's head and skull has no bearing on his or her personality.

This drawing illustrates the lines and divisions of the human skull that were used by phrenologists to study personality traits. Phrenology no longer is considered a valid science.
(© iStockphoto.com / "*Mark Strozier*")

have discovered that brain activity during REM sleep begins in the pons—a structure in the brainstem—and in neighboring midbrain areas. The pons sends signals to turn off the motor neurons in the spinal cord, which keep the body at rest. But for some people this signal function doesn't work properly, and they can get up, move around, and perform many activities while they are asleep. Sleepwalking (or sleeptalking, sleepeating, sleepcleaning-the-house, or whatever) can result.

SLEEPWALKING

It's uncommon for sleepwalkers to roam around with their eyes closed and arms outstretched, as you often see in movies and on television. Sleepwalkers almost always have their eyes open so they can move around without bumping into things. Their eyes may have a glazed look, though, and if people try to talk to them, the sleepwalkers' answers are usually slow. Sometimes they don't even respond to questions. People have been known to eat, bathe, dress, whistle, dance, and even drive cars while sleepwalking!

Sleepwalking itself is not dangerous, but accidents can happen when someone is sleepwalking, and in some cases supervision becomes necessary. The idea that you're not supposed to wake people while they are sleepwalking because it might shock or harm them is false. It's perfectly fine to rouse a sleepwalker and help him or her back to bed. In the case of a sleepdancer, the person may even thank you for it.

THE HUMAN BRAIN IS LIKE A SUPERCOMPUTER, ONLY BETTER. IT HAS BILLIONS OF INDIVIDUAL PIECES AND TRILLIONS OF DIFFERENT CONNECTIONS, WEIGHS ABOUT THREE POUNDS, AND RUNS ON ELECTROCHEMICAL ENERGY.

NIGHTMARES

What's the difference between a dream and a nightmare? A nightmare *is* a dream, but it's usually more intense and contains thoughts or images that are unpleasant to the sleeper. Not too long ago, nightmares were thought to be the work of demons that would come in the night and sit on the chests of sleeping people. At the turn of the last century a person's diet was believed to cause nightmares. Today people believe that nightmares occur in response to certain body functions, such as high fevers, or in response to various mental states, such as shock, upset, and stress. It isn't unusual for people to have a nightmare once in a while, but nightmares that occur frequently can interfere with a person's sleep.

LUCID DREAMING

Unlike nightmares and regular dreams, in what are called "lucid dreams," the sleeper is aware that he or she is dreaming and is conscious enough to take control of the dream. The sleeper can participate in and actually take charge of his or her dream and decide on the content and the quality of the experience— just like playing a character in a video game. Lucid dreams can feel especially vivid, depending on the sleeper's level of self-awareness within the dream. It is perhaps because of this fact that lucid dreams tend to be much more memorable than regular dreams.

Lucid dreams can begin from a sleep state—the sleeper starts out having a normal dream that then becomes lucid. Or a lucid dream can begin from a waking state, and the person lapses from alert reality into lucid dreaming. This second type of lucid dreaming is commonly recognized as hypnosis— a state that is somewhere between being awake and being asleep.

A number of universities, including Stanford University, are conducting studies of the causes and effects of lucid dreams. Among other benefits, there is some thought that people can learn to use lucid dreaming to relieve nightmares. Below is a list of common nightmares with suggestions for turning them around by training the brain to apply lucid dreaming.

Dream #1. *You're being chased by a monster,*
a person, or an animal.

What to do: Tell yourself to stop running. Consider turning around and facing whoever or whatever is chasing you. When you do this, the chaser usually becomes harmless. You also can try to talk to the chaser. In a dream, it's possible to talk to anyone or anything and to be as strong and brave as you imagine yourself to be.

Dream # 2. *You're falling.*

What to do: Pretend you're falling on purpose because you're a famous skydiver. Tell yourself that you have a parachute attached to your back and then pull the string. You'll

land safely, on target, to the cheers of your fellow skydivers. Another way to take charge of this nightmare is to tell yourself that you're flying instead of falling. Soar off and enjoy the sensation before landing on a field full of soft grass.

Dream #3. *You're stuck—*
you can't move.

What to do: First of all, don't panic. Take a deep breath and then slowly relax. This feeling of being frozen usually happens when your body is tense. If you will yourself to relax, the feeling will slowly fade away.

Dream #4. *You're unprepared for a big test*
or an important speech.

What to do: There are a couple of ways to handle this disturbing nightmare. First of all, you can ask to be excused from the classroom to make an important call home. Once you're out of the situation, the dream usually goes away. The second way is to admit—in the dream—that you forgot to prepare for the big speech, but tackle the rest of the speech anyway. Replace the fear with a bit of confidence and the dream can take a new direction.

AWAKENING THE BRAIN

The British-born neurologist Dr. Oliver Sacks came to New York in 1965 and began treating a group of patients with sleeping sickness at Beth Abraham Hospital. Sleeping sickness is a rare inflammation of the brain that struck in the 1920s for unknown reasons and then vanished. Sleeping sickness left patients in a frozen, comalike state from which many were unable to recover. Some of the patients Sacks worked with had been unable to move on their own for decades. Sacks treated the patients with

Neurologist Dr. Oliver Sacks stands in front of the Beth Abraham Hospital, where he helped patients frozen by sleeping sickness become "awake" and active.

an experimental drug called "L-dopa," and it had a surprising, transformative, and "awakening" effect. When the patients awoke, it became apparent that sleeping sickness had frozen time for some of them. A few still thought they were youngsters, and many of them had difficulty adapting to the modern world. For a majority of the patients, the "awakening" was only temporary, and within a short time these people fell back "asleep." Sacks documented his work in a best-selling book, *Awakenings*. In 1990, the book was made into an Oscar-nominated feature film.

Sacks continues to break new ground and experiment with different treatments for a variety of uncommon and unusual neurological conditions. He believes he has found a remedy as powerful and useful as L-dopa: music. He has studied music's profound effect on the brain, including its ability to restore memory and language to people who have disorders such as Parkinson's disease or have had strokes. He has worked with other patients who were unable to speak or move—until he introduced music.

Dr. Sacks speculates that the human brain is hardwired to respond to rhythms and musical beats. Using brain scans of people who have brain dysfunctions and other disorders, Sacks has observed that the brain circuits that respond to music are often intact—providing a vital link to people who may have lost the ability to communicate. During treatment, Sacks may start by singing simple, well-known songs such as "Happy Birthday" to the patient, even if it isn't his or her birthday. Surprisingly, patients who have lost the ability to speak often are able to regain sounds and words by singing. Although it requires intensive therapy, it is sometime possible for the patient to use singing as a means to begin speaking again. Sacks often works with elderly patients and finds that music from a person's own generations is particularly powerful and effective. One of his favorite songs to use is "A Bicycle Built for Two."

DISORDERS OF THE BRAIN

The brain can be a powerful friend, but this complex machine also can be a foe. People with mental disorders or mental illness can experience distress and disability. Mental illness is a disruption of mental processes or behavior patterns. For some people the episodes of disruption are brief, but for others the effects can last for a lifetime. Before modern treatment options were developed, sections of the brain were sliced apart in operations called "lobotomies." Lobotomies were thought to help people with mental disorders, but the procedure usually made the situation worse or radically changed the personality of the patient. Most doctors consider the procedure—first performed with an ice pick—to be "one of the most barbaric mistakes ever perpetrated by mainstream medicine." Over time, treatment options for mental illnesses have improved significantly. Advances in therapy and medication allow most people with mental illnesses to find comfort. Some common—and a few quite uncommon—mental disorders are described in the paragraphs that follow.

SACKS HAS OBSERVED THAT THE BRAIN CIRCUITS THAT RESPOND TO MUSIC ARE OFTEN INTACT—PROVIDING A VITAL LINK TO PEOPLE WHO MAY HAVE LOST THE ABILITY TO COMMUNICATE.

SCHIZOPHRENIA

Schizophrenia is a brain disorder that affects almost one in a hundred people around the world. Usually, it strikes during the late teenage and early adult years. For men, it tends to surface between the ages of fifteen and twenty-five—later for women, between ages twenty-five and thirty-five. Schizophrenia means "shattered mind," but it has nothing to do with a "split personality" or "multiple personalities." People with schizophrenia have a difficult time distinguishing between reality and fantasy. Sometimes they have hallucinations or experience delusions, and they often have difficulty talking. Quite often, schizophrenic people withdraw from society. Most medical authorities today believe that this condition is a result of genetic factors. Even though schizophrenia is not caused by stress or drug use, those factors can precipitate and worsen the illness. Today, schizophrenia can be treated medically with relatively high success rates, but the patient must remember to take the proper medications daily—or even several times a day—and so assistance is sometimes necessary.

DISSOCIATIVE IDENTITY DISORDER (FORMERLY CALLED "MULTIPLE PERSONALITY DISORDER")

Dissociative identity disorder is a clinical diagnosis that describes people who display more than one identity or personality (called "alter egos" or simply "alters"). Each of the personalities has a separate way of being in the world, and a person with this condition can undergo changes in his or her personality or switch identities in the space of just a few seconds. Although this condition is rare, it's a popular story line for books, television shows, and movies because it's so extreme.

The various personalities housed in the same person totally dominate and control the behavior of the individual. During routine jumps from one personality to the next, the individual experiences memory loss. These patients cannot remember being the person they were just a few moments earlier. The specific causes of dissociative identity disorder are still unknown. Exposure to traumatic experiences seems to contribute to its onset. Mental health professionals reason that the disorder is a defense mechanism. It helps a person cope with his or her personal problems if the burden can be shifted to another personality.

There are various treatment options available. Some methods are used to unite all the personalities. Other methods focus on working with one of the personalities specifically. But most professionals try to address the roots of the problems that led to the disorder. Some combination of talk therapy and medication is typical.

In 1957, two psychiatrists, Corbett Thigpen and Hervey Cleckley, published a book called *The Three Faces of Eve*. The story is loosely based on their experiences treating a woman named Chris Costner Sizemore—renamed "Eve White" for the book and a movie adaptation. Sizemore witnessed two deaths and a tragic accident in a short time span when she was a small child. Those events led her to be diagnosed with dissociative identity disorder and caused her to experience up to twenty different personalities at various periods in her life. In 1973 another book, *Sybil*, by Flora Rheta Schreiber detailed the story of a woman who had sixteen different personalities. Like *The Three Faces of Eve, Sybil* became a popular movie. Television shows and movies continue to keep the spotlight on dissociative identity disorder because it captures the viewer's imagination and makes for a great plot twist.

GILLE DE LA TOURETTE'S SYNDROME

Tourette's syndrome is a disorder that causes involuntary body movements—sudden motions such as twitches or spasms—and uncontrollable vocal sounds such as sudden outbursts of noise or language. Tourette's is just one of many tic disorders, which can be either temporary or permanent.

Tourette's once was considered a rare and bizarre disorder and is best known for obscene outbursts—people shouting dirty words or saying things best left unspoken. We now know that this "potty mouth" symptom only affects a small percentage of people with Tourette's. But researchers have discovered that Tourette's is more common than once was believed—especially in children. It's estimated that between one and ten of every thousand children are affected with Tourette's to some degree. Many outgrow the disorder once they reach adolescence, but some do not.

The exact cause of Tourette's is unknown, but genetics and environmental factors are suspected to play a role. These are no known treatments, and many believe that medication for the disorder is unnecessary because Tourette's does not affect life expectancy or intelligence. Several famous people—including the author Samuel Johnson—are suspected of having had Tourette's.

FAMOUS BRAINS

The famous English poet Lord Byron had an enormous brain. It weighed six pounds, which is double the size of the average human brain. For centuries, scientists have been trying to figure out if there's a relationship between brain size and intelligence. Popular opinion assumed that a bigger brain made for a smarter person, but two specific brains disproved that theory. After their deaths, the brains of Albert Einstein, the famous physicist, and Walt Whitman, the famous American poet, were removed and examined. The brains of those two geniuses were discovered to be smaller than average.

Still, researchers refused to give up their search for physical evidence of intellect—some even refused to give up the famous brains themselves. Dr. Thomas Harvey was on call the night of April 17, 1955, when Einstein died at Princeton Hospital in New Jersey. Harvey performed an autopsy and removed Einstein's brain—against the wishes outlined in his will—before the physicist was cremated. A few months after the autopsy, Harvey was fired from the hospital because he refused to part with Einstein's brain.

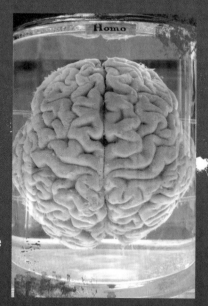

Even though he was not a brain specialist and had no special research skills, Harvey kept the brain—stored inside two jars of formaldehyde—in his basement. He routinely promised the media that he was just one year away from sharing

A photograph of a real human brain preserved in a formaldehyde solution.
(© iStockphoto.com / "Baloncici")

the results of his research on the brain, but no report was issued. Over the next forty years Harvey lost his medical license, moved to the Midwest, and even embarked on a cross-country trip to deliver the brain to Einstein's granddaughter (who didn't want it) before finally returning the brain to its original location in Princeton Hospital.

Scientists who later examined Einstein's brain counted the number of neurons (cells that process and transmit information) and neuroglia (cells that provide support and protection for the neurons by supplying them with nutrients and oxygen) in the four areas of Einstein's brain. They discovered that Einstein's brain had more neuroglia cells for every neuron cell than did the other brains they had studied. Their conclusion was that the neurons in Einstein's brain needed and used more energy and that this may have led to better thinking and conceptual skills.

PHINEAS GAGE

One of the most famous and most baffling stories about the brain in history is that of Phineas Gage. Phineas was a railroad construction foreman. On September 13, 1848, he and his crew were working outside the small town of Cavendish, Vermont. One of Phineas's jobs was to set explosive charges into holes that had been drilled into large rocks so that the rocks could be exploded, broken up, and removed to make way for new railway lines. One day a distracted Phineas filled the hole in a rock with gunpowder and added a fuse but forgot to pack the hole with a protective layer of sand. When he went to compress the nonex-istent sand with his tamping iron, the tamping iron sparked against the rock and ignited the gunpowder. The force of the resulting explosion was so great that it sent the tamping iron all the way through Phineas's skull. The rod entered through the side of Phineas's face above his jaw and exited out of the top of his head. It knocked him out, but it didn't kill him.

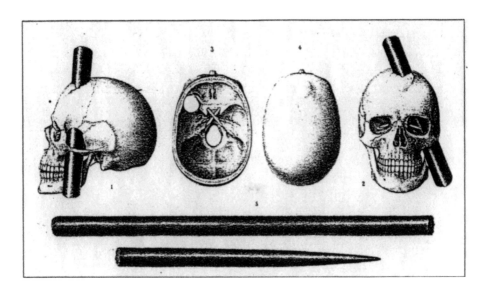

This drawing of Phineas Gage's skull details the location of the iron tamping rod that was rocketed through his head—yet miraculously did not kill him.
(AP Photo / Courtesy of Harvard Medical School)

THE FORCE OF THE RESULTING EXPLOSION WAS SO GREAT THAT IT SENT THE TAMPING IRON ALL THE WAY THROUGH PHINEAS'S SKULL. IT KNOCKED HIM OUT, BUT IT DIDN'T KILL HIM.

Remarkably, Phineas regained consciousness within a few minutes. He was able to speak and survived a forty-five-minute ride in a cart back to his boardinghouse—even though he had a giant hole in his head. He was treated by the doctors Edward H. Williams and John Martyn Harlow and remained in their care until April 1849.

Despite having an iron bar launched through his head, Phineas sustained surprisingly little physical damage. He lost the sight in his left eye, and he also had some facial disfigurement and paralysis. Phineas soon returned to work on the railroad, but his personality began to change in some ways. Before the accident, he had been hardworking, responsible, and popular with his crew. After the accident, he started using profanity, showed little regard for the men in his crew, and couldn't get along with his superiors. It wasn't long before he was fired from his job with the railroad.

Phineas joined P.T. Barnum's circus for a brief period as a sideshow attraction. When his health started to fail in 1859, he went to San Francisco to live with his mother and sister. He recovered briefly under their care but began to have convulsions and finally died in 1860—just fewer than twelve years after his accident. In 1866 Dr. Harlow removed Phineas's head from his grave site with the permission of his family. According to Harlow, Phineas was given the rod that went through his head a year after his accident. Phineas gave the rod to Harvard University but reclaimed it and carried it with him until his death. Harlow took both the skull and the rod, wrote a paper about Phineas's accident, and placed both on display at the

Harvard Medical School's Warren Anatomical Museum, where they can be viewed today.

Though the date and spelling of his name are incorrect and the extent of his recovery somewhat exaggerated, the rod was engraved with the following description:

> *This is the bar that was shot through the head of Mr. Phineluis P. Gage at Cavendish, Vermont, Sept. 14, 1848. He fully recovered from the injure & deposited this bar in the Museum of the Medical College, Harvard University. Phinehaus P. Gage Jan 6 1850.*

For scientists working with the brain, Phineas's case is very significant. It offered the first evidence that damage to the frontal brain lobes can alter a person's personality significantly. Before Phineas's accident, scientists thought the frontal lobes played no role in a person's behavior.

VIRULENT VIRUSES: RARE AND HORRIBLE
4. DISEASES

A virus is a very small infectious agent that can multiply only with the help of a host—living cells of humans, animals, or plants and bacteria. These little freeloaders generally cause great harm to the host they depend on. The diseases Ebola, West Nile, and avian influenza (or bird flu)—all of which you want to avoid contracting—are caused by some of the most deadly and feared viruses known to modern medicine.

EBOLA

In April 1995, a man checked himself into a hospital in Kikwit, a town in the southern part of the Democratic Republic of Congo in Africa. He told the doctor that he was suffering from severe diarrhea and had a very high fever. At first, the doctor assumed that the man had dysentery because it is such a common disease in that part of the world, but when the man began to bleed from his ears, eyes, and mouth, the doctor realized that the situation was much more serious.

It soon was discovered that the man's internal organs had turned to liquid, and he died. Several members of the medical staff who had been treating the man also became seriously ill and died. The residents of Kikwit fled the city in terror, but in doing so they carried the strange illness to nearby towns and villages. Soon, the people there began to die as well. The government in the capital city, Kinshasa, sent in the army to set up barricades on all roads leading out of the area to contain the outbreak and protect the rest of the country.

The World Health Organization sent in a team of specialists. The members of the team wore special suits to keep themselves safe while they investigated and studied samples from infected villagers. They discovered that the virus responsible for the outbreak was one that hadn't been observed since 1976, when it killed several hundred people in northern Congo. The virus was called "Ebola," named after the Ebola River—the site where the first recognized case of Ebola occurred. The virus is found primarily in the tropical forests of Africa.

The Ebola virus is thought to originate in animals and is transmitted from an infected animal to a human being. Once the virus infects a human being, it can spread from person to person through direct contact with body fluids such as blood and saliva. There are no treatments or vaccines for the Ebola virus. If a person is infected with Ebola, generally he or she will have fever, severe headache, chills, sore throat, joint and muscle pain, a feeling of extreme weakness, and dizziness within just a few days. These symptoms are associated with a wide variety of diseases, so early detection of Ebola can be difficult. As the disease progresses, organ damage and internal bleeding can occur. The death rate for those with Ebola is high, and in its final stages it can cause people to bleed from the nose, mouth, eyes, and ears.

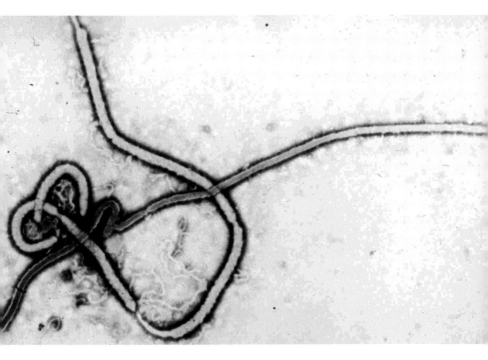

This is a photograph of the Ebola virus taken by the Centers for Disease Control and Prevention on May 11, 1995. The virus strain pictured was responsible for the deaths in the Kikwit outbreak. (AP PHOTO / HO, CDC)

However, for reasons we have yet to uncover, some people do recover from Ebola. The recovery is slow, though, and it typically takes many months for a person to regain his or her weight and strength. For most people, the possibility of contracting the Ebola virus is very low. Exposure is limited to those areas of the world where outbreaks have occurred, such as Angola, the Democratic Republic of Congo, Gabon, Ivory Coast, and Sudan.

BIOCONTAINMENT

Specialized laboratories are necessary to study viruses and microorganisms such as bacteria. If the material being studied could pose a health hazard to either the researcher or other people in the immediate area, various levels of laboratory safety are put into place. These safety measures are called "biocontainment." Each laboratory is assigned a biosafety level (BSL) that is based on the type of work being done and its potential threat. BSL-I is the lowest danger level, and BSL-4 is the highest.

A BSL-I laboratory typically is found at a university and is used mostly for teaching microbiology. The materials being used are known not to cause disease in healthy humans. The safety features in this type of laboratory include wearing lab coats and washing the hands before and after working with the microorganisms. Most of the work is done on open-air tables without specialized equipment to contain the organisms. There are no particular entry or exit restrictions for the laboratory.

A BSL-2 laboratory is similar to a BSL-I lab, but there are additional safety features in place, including trained personnel wearing sterile gloves to allow for the study of microorganisms that could be hazardous to human health, such as measles. Special protective clothing, such as a face mask, is always worn during experiments. Access to this type of laboratory is restricted while work is being conducted, and everyone who works in the lab, including students, is tested regularly for any signs of infection.

A BSL-3 laboratory is a facility for working with microorganisms that could easily become airborne and that carry a high risk of infection, such as the West Nile virus. These laboratories usually are found either in hospitals or at a research facility for infectious diseases. In addition to the safety features of BSL-I and BSL-2 laboratories, a BSL-3 facility has more restricted access. Often, there are double doors that are sealed around their edges, and the first door must be closed before the second door can be opened. The ventilation system is separate from the rest of the building. The air from the laboratory is filtered to remove any microorganisms before it is released outside. These labs are monitored on a regular basis by government inspectors.

A BSL-4 laboratory is designed for work with the most infectious microorganisms known to science: the Ebola virus, Bacillus anthracis (which causes anthrax), the Marburg virus, and hantavirus, to name just a few. BLS-4 labs also study viruses that have no known treatments or vaccines. Entry to this type of laboratory is gained only through passages that have several checkpoints and security codes that are issued only after a person has been vaccinated against the microorganisms being studied. All work is done in pressurized and ventilated suits. Filtered air for breathing is piped into the suit through a hose. To prevent contamination, the lab is kept at negative air pressure, which means that if an outside barrier such as a wall or window is broken, air will flow only into the lab, not out of the lab. These laboratories are completely separate from other facilities. They are fenced, equipped with observation cameras, and heavily guarded.

A BSL-4 LABORATORY IS DESIGNED FOR WORK WITH THE MOST INFECTIOUS MICROORGANISMS KNOWN TO SCIENCE: THE EBOLA VIRUS, BACILLUS ANTHRACIS (WHICH CAUSES ANTHRAX), THE MARBURG VIRUS, AND HANTAVIRUS.

WEST NILE VIRUS

In the summer of 2000, New York City's Central Park was closed to the public temporarily because mosquitoes carrying the potentially deadly West Nile virus were discovered in the area. An open-air concert that would have attracted up to 40,000 people was canceled so that the park could be sprayed with insecticides. Mayor Rudolph Giuliani called on everyone in the city to stay calm, but the closure of the large park—situated right in the middle of densely populated Manhattan—caused more than a few people to flee the city.

The West Nile virus causes swelling of the brain and is accompanied by fever, headache, body ache, skin rashes, and swollen lymph glands. The virus mainly kills birds and certain other animals, but it caused a panic when it entered the United States in 1999 and killed seven people in New York City. Although the West Nile virus is transmitted by mosquitoes, the main carriers are birds—especially crows, robins, and blue jays. If a mosquito bites a bird that is infected with the West Nile virus, the virus enters the mosquito's bloodstream and eventually settles in its salivary glands. When that mosquito bites a human being, the virus enters the human's bloodstream. Infection usually takes place during warm weather months, when mosquitoes are active. The time between the bite and the appearance of West Nile virus symptoms can range from two to fourteen days. Those infected with the virus may experience only minor skin rashes, headaches, and nausea, but others can have more severe reactions, including coma, convulsions, partial paralysis, and inflammation of the brain, all of which are life-threatening. Despite the dangers, many people recover from West Nile virus—even those who develop serious symptoms can be treated and cured with intravenous fluids and pain relievers.

Since the introduction of the West Nile virus into the United States, it has appeared in all forty-eight of the contiguous states, but the virus is most common in Africa, the Middle East, and western Asia. The very first strain of the virus is thought to date back to the 1600s, so even though we've seen the virus spread in recent years, humans have been coexisting successfully with the West Nile virus for hundreds of years.

Mosquitoes, like the one photographed here, carry and transmit the West Nile virus. (© iStockphoto.com / "Douglas Allen")

GROSS! FLESH-EATING BACTERIA

Bacteria—very small microscopic organisms—tend to be harmless. In fact, they are essential to the world's ecosystem, because they help decompose the things around us— including garbage—allowing for new growth. But lurking in this group are a few bad eggs.

In 2001, a mechanic in California went to a local hospital after he was injured on the job. He was given an MRI scan (a magnetic resonance imaging scan is similar to an X-ray but shows muscles and organs more clearly) and then sent home. Two days later, he went to the emergency room in the middle of the night because he was feeling violently ill. While he was sitting in a wheelchair, he blacked out. When he finally awakened two days later, he was in the intensive care unit with a bandage covering his right arm. He later learned that he had contracted necrotizing fasciitis, commonly known as "flesh-eating bacteria," a rare and severe infection that releases toxins that cause the destruction of skin and muscle.

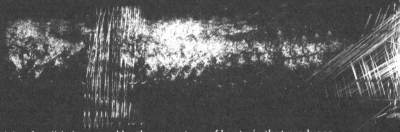

Necrotizing fasciitis is caused by the same type of bacteria that produces strep throat and skin infections such as impetigo. A lot of people carry the bacteria in their throat or on their skin but show no signs of illness. Very few people who come in contact with the bacteria will develop necrotizing fasciitis. The bacteria can enter the body through a scratch, a blister, or some other minor skin injury. Tissue removal and antibiotics are the two most common treatment methods—early detection is also key. If not caught in time, necrotizing fasciitis can be fatal.

BIRD FLU

Avian influenza, more commonly known as "bird flu," has claimed the lives of millions of birds—and those of a few humans, too. Wild birds carry the virus but usually do not get sick. This virus, however, is fatal for domestic birds such as chickens, ducks, and turkeys. The migration of wild birds contributes to the infection of domestic birds. It's relatively difficult for humans to contract the disease, and those who do get it have been in close contact with infected birds. There have been a few cases in which humans have passed the illness to one another, and this human-to-human transmission concerns health officials all over the world. If the bird flu virus, known as "H5N1," ever mutates, or transforms, into a form that can pass more easily from one human to another, there could be a worldwide flu epidemic like the pandemic of 1918 and 1919, which killed millions.

Chicken coops, like the one in this photograph, that house domestic birds can become infected with avian influenza, or bird flu. (© iSTOCKPHOTO.COM / "McKEVIN SHAUGHNESSY")

IF THE BIRD FLU VIRUS,
EVER MUTATES INTO A
FORM THAT CAN PASS
MORE EASILY FROM ONE
HUMAN TO ANOTHER,
THERE COULD BE A
WORLDWIDE FLU EPIDEMIC
LIKE THE PANDEMIC OF
1918 AND 1919, WHICH
KILLED MILLIONS.

In humans, it's unknown how long it takes for bird flu to develop, but health professionals estimate one to five days after initial exposure. At first, bird flu is difficult to differentiate from conventional flu, because the symptoms are similar, including cough, fever, sore throat, and muscle aches and pains. Eye infections such as conjunctivitis sometimes accompany bird flu in humans. When treated early, people usually recover from bird flu with the help of prescription medications. If the disease progresses untreated, viral pneumonia may occur, and it is this respiratory distress that is the most common cause of death.

A 1997 outbreak of bird flu in Hong Kong infected eighteen people, six of whom later died. Since that time, human cases of the bird flu have been reported in Asia, Europe, and the Middle East. Health officials in those areas were able to confirm that most of the cases involved people who had contact with infected domestic poultry or visited areas that had been contaminated by wild birds. Flu viruses also can originate in areas where people raise pigs because pigs are susceptible to both bird and human viruses. If a pig is infected by a bird, the pig's body becomes a type of "virus mixing bowl," and the pig then can transmit that virus to a human being.

Researchers around the world are working tirelessly to develop a vaccine that will protect people from an outbreak. In 2007 researchers in Singapore announced that they have developed a handheld device that analyzes the results from a throat swab to detect bird flu immediately. Early detection measures such as these can help save lives.

ANIMALS HELP OUT
Avian flu is for the birds, but could a rat save your life?

For most people, rats are associated with filth, disease, and the destruction of food crops, but in East Africa, specifically in Tanzania, the African giant pouched rat is being trained and used to sniff out life-threatening tuberculosis (TB) bacteria in samples of saliva taken from residents in that country's poorest neighborhoods. In recent trials, the rats correctly identified 300 cases of TB in its earliest stages—cases that had been missed by lab technicians using microscopes. This type of early detection can save hundreds of lives. A single rat can diagnose up to 2,000 saliva samples a day, whereas a laboratory technician usually can diagnose only about 20. At first, many international agencies called the use of rats ridiculous, but now the project has the backing of both the World Bank and the United Nation. Bart Weetjens, the Belgian scientist who conceived the program, calls the rats "organized, sensitive, sociable, and smart" and says that since rats don't form emotional attachments to a single handler, as do dogs, for instance, they'll work happily with anyone as long as they are rewarded with a few peanuts or a ripe banana for their efforts.

MEDICAL MARVELS CAN
5. HAPPEN TO YOU!

When you look in the mirror, you probably don't see a face full of hair like Jo-Jo the Dog-Faced Boy. It's unlikely that you ran wild in the forests of Africa with a band of vervet monkeys. The local museum doesn't display a large metal rod that traveled through your brain. Chances are that you've never had Ebola, either. But don't feel left out. You're still a medical marvel.

YOUR "FUNNY" BONE

Have you ever bumped the inside of your elbow and felt a prickly kind of pain? That's your "funny" bone, but it really isn't a bone. It's a *nerve*, and it makes your arm tingle and feel, well, *funny*. So what's going on? The ulnar nerve runs down the inside of your elbow. It controls your fourth and fifth fingers and also the movement of your wrist. That funny feeling happens when the ulnar nerve is bumped against the humerus (get it? *humorous?*), which is the long bone that starts at the elbow and goes up to the shoulder. Nothing bad happens to this nerve when you hit it—it just feels funny.

YAWNING

Look around you no matter where you are—at school, in the mall, or at home. If you can find somebody who's yawning, wait

YAWNING IS AN
INVOLUNTARY REFLEX.
WHY DOES THIS HAPPEN?
HONESTLY, NOBODY
KNOWS FOR SURE,
BUT WE DO KNOW
THAT EVERYONE—
FROM UNBORN BABIES
TO GREAT-GRANDPARENTS
AND EVEN ANIMALS—
YAWNS.

to see how long it takes for you to do the same thing. Or just think about yawning, and you'll yawn. Yawning is an involuntary reflex. Why does this happen? Honestly, nobody knows for sure, but we do know that *everyone*—from unborn babies to great-grandparents and even animals—yawns.

Some scientific studies suggest that yawning happens when we are bored or tired because we don't breathe as deeply as we should, which means our bodies take in less oxygen. Yawning helps the body bring more oxygen into the blood and get rid of carbon dioxide. But there are other theories. Some scientists think that yawning helps us stretch parts of the body, such as the lungs, muscles, and joints. They think it helps increase the heart rate and makes us feel more awake. Still others think yawning is a way to redistribute an oil-like substance called "surfactant," which helps keep the lungs lubricated so that we can breathe more easily. If the lungs were dry, it would become difficult to breathe. But there is one thing we know for sure about yawning—it's contagious.

SNEEZING

Sneezing is the body's way of getting rid of something that is irritating the inside of the nose. Sneezing is also called "sternutation." When there's something tickling the inside of the nose, a message is sent to the so-called sneeze center of the brain. That center then sends a message to all the muscles to work together to create the complicated reaction that we call a sneeze. Those muscles are in the stomach, the chest, just below the lungs, the vocal cords, the back of the throat, and the *eyelids*—because we always close our eyes when we sneeze. All these muscles function in unison to launch

This photograph captures a sneeze against a black background to illustrate the spray droplets—which can be launched at speeds up to 150 feet per second—emitted from the nose and mouth. (AP Photo)

the irritation out of your nose at up to 100 miles per hour. Of course, it's important that you hold a handkerchief or a tissue in front of your nose when you sneeze so that you won't send something across the room and hit one of your friends. If you don't have a handkerchief or a tissue handy, get your hand up there as fast as you can, but then excuse yourself to go wash it.

A lot of things can irritate your nose and cause you to sneeze: dust, cold air, pepper, pet dander (tiny scales from an animal's

A LOT OF THINGS CAN CAUSE YOU TO SNEEZE: DUST, COLD AIR, PEPPER, PET DANDER, AND POLLEN FROM PLANTS. SOME PEOPLE EVEN SNEEZE WHEN THEY STEP OUT INTO THE SUNLIGHT.

hair or skin), and pollen from plants. Some people even sneeze when they step out into the sunlight. If you've ever had the feeling that you were about to sneeze but then it just got stuck and wouldn't come out, all you need to do is look briefly toward a bright light (but don't stare at it and don't look right into the sun), and your sneeze probably will come unstuck.

"BRAIN FREEZE"

Have you ever wondered why you get a headache when you eat or drink something cold? Ice cream, slushy frozen drinks, and even cold soda, water, milk, or juice can do it. When whatever it is you're eating or drinking touches the roof of your mouth, which is called the "palate," it can affect certain nerves that control how much blood flows to your head. Those nerves respond to the cold by signaling the blood vessels in your head to swell. This sudden swelling causes your head to pound and hurt. A lot of people call this "brain freeze," but rest assured that nothing is really happening in your brain at all. These headaches don't last long—about five minutes at the most—and when that pain goes away, it's usually followed by a wonderful feeling of relief.

Brain freeze isn't dangerous, and nothing is wrong with your body. But if you'd rather avoid it, there are things you can do. Try to eat slowly and try to warm the food you're eating or drinking in the front part of your mouth before you swallow it. If you do feel a headache coming on, you may be able to slow it down a bit by holding your tongue against your palate. This will warm the palate and allow you to enjoy the rest of your treat.

CONCLUSION

Our investigation of medical marvels has led us around the world and introduced us to scores of fascinating people. We solved a few cases, but many more will require further evidence and continued exploration. What happed to the gazelle boy after Armen lost all trace of him in the Sahara Desert? Was he ever there to begin with, or was he a figment of Armen's imagination? Why do we dream? Will Einstein's brain ever give up the secret to his genius? How and when will we discover a vaccine for bird flu? Will disease-sniffing rats gain popularity and help people receive lifesaving early treatment?

We can only hope curious minds like yours will stay on the case and help solve these mysteries.

CHAPTER NOTES

The following notes consist of citations to the sources of quoted material. Each citation includes the first and last words or phrases of the quotation and its source. References are to works cited in the Sources, beginning on page 84.

BOGDAN——*FREAK SHOW: PRESENTING HUMAN ODDITIES FOR AMUSEMENT AND PROFIT*

Boston——www.boston.com/news/science/articles/2008/ 11/2/mankinds_new_best_friend/?page=1

Macmillan——*An Odd Kind of Fame: Stories of Phineas Gage*

Kipling——*The Jungle Book*

Kunstkamera——www.kunstkamera.ru/en/history/encyclopedia _of_peters_kunstkammer/the_first_russian_museum/

PBS——*The Lobotomist*

CHAPTER ONE: CIRCUS CHARADE: RARE MEDICAL CONDITIONS

PAGE

2   "artistic human creations." Kunstkamera

6   "By special permit . . . effected. . . ." Bogdan, pages 98–100

CHAPTER TWO: BORN TO BE WILD

PAGE

19–20   "Baloo was teaching him . . .all the law of the Jungle." Kipling, pages 27–28.

CHAPTER THREE: MARVELOUS MACHINE: THE BRAIN

PAGE

47   "one of the most . . . medicine." PBS

57   "This is the bar . . . 1850." Macmillan, page 47

CHAPTER FOUR: VIRULENT VIRUSES: RARE AND HORRIBLE DISEASES

PAGE

73   "organized, sensitive, sociable, and smart." Boston

SOURCES

BOOKS:

Armen, Jean-Claude. *Gazelle-Boy: A Child Brought Up by Gazelles in the Sahara Desert*. London: Bodley Head, 1974.

Bogdan, Robert. *Freak Show: Presenting Human Oddities for Amusement and Profit*. Chicago: University of Chicago Press, 1988.

Butcher, Nancy. *The Strange Case of the Walking Corpse*. New York: Avery, 2004.

Fleischman, John. *Phineas Gage: A Gruesome but True Story about Brain Science*. Boston: Houghton Mifflin, 2002.

Hornberger, Francine. *Carny Folk: The World's Weirdest Side Show Acts*. New York: Citadel Press, 2005.

Kipling, Rudyard. *The Jungle Book*. New York: Sterling, 2007.

Macmillan, Malcolm. *An Odd Kind of Fame: Stories of Phineas Gage*. Cambridge, MA: MIT Press, 2000

Newton, Michael. *Savage Girls and Wild Boys: A History of Feral Children*. New York: Thomas Dunne Books/St. Martin's Press, 2003.

ARTICLES:

BBC Online Network. "From Monkey Boy to Choir Boy." October 6, 1999. www.news.bbc.co.uk/1/hi/uk/466616.stm.

Behegan, David. "Author Admits Making Up Memoir of Surviving Holocaust." *Boston Globe*, February 29, 2008.

Native American Facts for Kids. "Sac and Fox Indian Fact Sheet." www.bigorrin.org/sf_kids.htm(accessed November 2008).

Vash, Carolyn L. "Disability Attitudes for All Latitudes." *Journal of Rehabilitation*, 2001. www.thefreelibrary.com/Changing+attitudes+toward+ people+with+disabilities.

World Health Organization. "Lymphatic Filariasis." Fact Sheet Number 102. September 2000.

ONLINE RESOURCES:

www.barnum-museum.org

www.boston.com/news/science/articles/2008/11/23/
        mankinds_new_best_friend/?page=1

www.cdc.gov/od/ohs/biosfty/primary_containment_for_biohazards.pdf

www.faculty.washington.edu/chudler/ein.html

www.kunstkamera.ru/en/history/encyclopedia_of_peters_kunstkammer/
        the_first_russian_museum/

www.lib.unc.edu.ncc.gallery/twins.html

www.mayoclinic.com/health/bird-flu/DS00566

www.mayoclinic.com/health/cellulitis/DS00450

www.mayoclinic.com/health/conjoined-twins/DS00869

www.mayoclinic.com/health/ebola-virus/DS00996

www.mayoclinic.com/health/west-nile-virus/DS00438

www.newsvote.bbc.co.uk/mpapps/pagetools/print/news.bbc.co.uk/2/
        hi/health/3486559.stm

www.nlm.nih.gov/hmd/conjoined

www.npr.org/templates/story/story.php?storyId=4602913

www.proteus-syndrome.org

www.ringling.com

www.timesonline.co.uk/tol/news/health/article2846843.ece

FILM

The Lobotomist. PBS: American Experience, 2008

INDEX